REAL-LIFE HAUNTINGS

BY DON ROFF

WHO GOES THERE?

A strange flash of light appears across the moonless sky. Mysterious and unexplained footsteps awaken you in the midnight hour—but no one is there. Is it the wind? The settling of the house? Or something else? It seems everyone has his or her own account of unexplained phenomenon.

Whether it was supernatural, like that of a ghost, is unknown and can probably never be explained. Only you can theorize if it was a natural occurrence or a supernatural one.

STRANGE BUT TRUE!

Have you had a supernatural experience? There's a slim but possible chance that you might have.

Maybe a ghostly form has visited you while you were sleeping? Maybe you or someone you know has received a message from a long-dead relative or loved one? Maybe you have lived in a haunted house?

If so, you are not alone. People all over have claimed such haunting phenomena and spectral events.

This book is an overview of the unexplained. It presents information based on the accounts of those who witnessed the events. The author's purpose is to suggest some possible explanations—but not necessarily the only ones—to these mysteries.

HOW TO USE THIS BOOK

On the bottom right side of every page, you will find a tab with instructions. These tabs will instruct you to pull out corresponding numbered slides and place them into your "ghost viewer." The three-dimensional images will enhance your ghostly experience of the book.

THE HORROR IN AMITYVILLE

What caused George and Kathy Lutz to uproot their family and flee their new house after 28 days, leaving all of their possessions behind? Apparently, evil spirits were the cause.

MOVING IN TO AMITYVILLE

In December 1975, George and Kathy Lutz bought a colonial-style home on 112 Ocean Drive in Amityville, New York. The house was empty for almost a year.

A year earlier, on November 13, 1974, Ronald DeFeo, age 24, shot his parents and four young brothers and sisters to death. Later, he claimed that "evil spirits" told him to do it.

STRANGE EVENTS OCCUR

The Lutzes bought the house because it was offered at a cheap price. However, soon after they moved in, the family claimed they immediately began to experience strange things.

The Lutz's five-year-old daughter, Missy, said she had an imaginary friend named "Jodie"—

POLICE LINE DO NOT C

who was a pig-like creature with glowing red eyes. Later, cloven footprints, like that from a pig, were found outside, in the snow, near the windows of the house. When George checked out the boathouse late one night, he saw glowing red eyes watch him from Missy's room.

Kathy reported having the feeling of "being embraced" by an unseen force when she was alone. She also discovered a small hidden room behind some shelving in the basement. Called "The Red Room" because of its bloody color, the mysterious space wasn't on any of the home's blueprints. The Lutz's dog, Harry, would not go near the room—he whined and cowered from it.

The Lutzes also experienced "cold spots," strange music that sounded like a "German marching band tuning up," phantom smells like perfume and rot, flies swarming in the house in the middle of winter, and green slime that dripped from the walls in the hall and from the keyhole in the playroom in the attic.

IMPACT OF THE HAUNTING

There have been many bestselling books, news articles, and several Hollywood movies about the horrifying events that allegedly surround the famous house in Amityville. Many people have sought to disclaim the Lutz's testimony as untrue.

Theories about what happened are still explored and argued today. The case of the Amityville Horror is one of the most popular—and profitable—hauntings of all time.

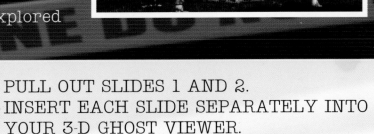

PULL OUT SLIDES 1 AND 2. INSERT EACH SLIDE SEPARATELY INTO YOUR 3-D GHOST VIEWER.

THE WINCHESTER HOUSE

In San Jose, California, stands one of the strangest homes ever built. This mysterious mansion was constantly being built upon, around the clock, for 38 years. Why was there so much construction on this sprawling estate? It is said that the ghosts wanted it that way.

THE SOUNDS OF GUNS AND GHOSTS

The mansion is renowned for its gargantuan size and sheer lack of any master building plan. According to popular belief, ghosts of individuals killed by Winchester Rifles haunted the house. Only continuous construction of the massive home would appease them.

Sarah Winchester, widow of Winchester Rifles tycoon William Wirt Winchester, used the millions of dollars she inherited from her husband's death to hire contractors to work day and night on the house.

When Sarah Winchester died in 1922, construction on the ever-growing mansion abruptly stopped.

A WEB OF ROOMS

Approximately 160 rooms—including 40 bedrooms and two ballrooms, one completed and one under construction—occupy the sprawling estate. The house also has 47 fireplaces, 10,000 window panes, 17 chimneys (with evidence of two others), two basements, and three elevators.

Spirits are said to have directly inspired the widow Winchester as to how the house should be built.

The number 13 and spider web motifs, which had spiritual meaning to the widow, appear around the house. For example, a chandelier that originally had 12 candleholders was altered to contain 13 candles, wall clothes hooks are in multiples of 13, and a spider web-patterned stained glass window contains 13 colored stones. Even the sink's drain covers have 13 holes.

The house, located on 525 South Winchester Boulevard, is now a popular tourist attraction, particularly during Halloween.

DOOR TO NOWHERE

HOUSE OF MYSTERY

t top: Spider-web designs decorate the macabre Winchester House windows.

At bottom: The bizarre "Door to owhere." Was it designed by ghosts?

PULL OUT SLIDES 3 AND 4. INSERT EACH SLIDE SEPARATELY INTO YOUR 3-D GHOST VIEWER.

FLIGHT OF THE MOTHMAN

In the mid-1960s, a creature was seen around Charleston and Point Pleasant, West Virginia. Witnesses described it as man-sized, with glowing red eyes and the wings of a moth. It had an unusual shriek that could be heard from a mile away. The creature apparently had great strength as well, as it was reportedly seen lifting extremely heavy objects, like cars.

THE MOTHMAN COMETH

The creature, later called the "Mothman," was first seen on the evening of November 12, 1966, by two couples driving out by an abandoned World War II explosives factory. They noticed two red lights hanging near the factory gate.

They discovered that the "lights" were the glowing red eyes of a large animal, "shaped like a man, but bigger, maybe six and a half or seven feet tall, with big wings folded against its back," according to one of the witnesses.

Terrified, they sped off down the road, but the creature supposedly chased their car—at speeds of over 100 miles per hour. The frightened couples headed to the nearest police station to describe the shocking event they had witnessed.

MYSTERIOUS MOTHMAN

Next page: The rebuilt Silver Bridge.

Above and right: A statue of the Mothman. What was it?

THE MOTHMAN PROPHECIES

Days later, many eyewitnesses described a similar creature: a large dark form with glowing eyes and a wide wingspan lurking around the abandoned explosives factory.

A year later, on December 15, 1967, the Mothman was sighted again just before the collapse of the Silver Bridge during rush-hour traffic—where 46 people died.

The Silver Bridge, named for its aluminum paint, was a suspension bridge that connected Point Pleasant to the state of Ohio over the Ohio River. The collapse of the bridge, built in 1928, was due to a manufacturing flaw.

A replacement bridge was built two years later.

Rumors spread that the Mothman would appear before upcoming disasters, as if trying to warn people.

After the collapse of the Silver Bridge, the Mothman was never again seen in Point Pleasant.

PULL OUT SLIDES 5 AND 6.
INSERT EACH SLIDE SEPARATELY INTO
YOUR 3-D GHOST VIEWER.

CURSE OF THE BELL WITCH

One of the greatest hauntings ever recorded, the Bell Witch has inspired many bestselling books and successful movie adaptations. Even US President Andrew Jackson was convinced that the Bell farm was haunted by a mean-spirited spook.

ATTACK OF THE WITCH

In Tennessee in 1817, John Bell was walking through his cornfield when he came across a strange creature that had the body of a dog and the head of a rabbit. He shot at it with a rifle but missed.

That night, the Bell family heard strange "beating" sounds outside the walls of their home. When they investigated the noises, no one was there.

Later, the family had their pillows and sheets thrown off their beds in the night while they slept. Betsy, the youngest member of the Bell family, reported being slapped or hit by an unseen force that left marks on her face.

The voice of an old woman could be heard laughing or crying, and even reciting church sermons that were given miles apart from one another.

General Jackson, who would later become president, investigated the haunting in 1819. John Bell tried unsuccessfully to keep the haunting secret.

Soon after arriving at the Bell farm, the general and his party left in great haste, frightened by the supernatural events they saw and heard.

Queen of the Haunted Dell.

TENNESSEE WITC
Detail from a 19
century engrav
of the infamou
Bell Witch.

3C 38
BELL WITCH
To the north was the farm of John Bell, an early, prominent settler from North Carolina. According to legend, his family was harried during the early 19th century by the famous Bell Witch. She kept the household in turmoil, assaulted Bell, and drove off Betsy Bell's suitor. Even Andrew Jackson who came to investigate, retreated to Nashville after his coach wheels stopped mysteriously. Many visitors to the house saw the furniture crash about them and heard her shriek, sing, and curse.

A DEATH IN THE FAMILY

One particularly disturbing occurrence was the death of John Bell, who reportedly drank a vial containing a poisonous liquid. The witch was later heard to say, "I gave ol' Jack a big dose of that last night and that fixed him!"

WITCHY PREDICTIONS

Soon after John Bell died, the hauntings tapered off. The last haunting was reported in 1828, when the witch returned to talk about life on earth and religion. She even made predictions about the Civil War, World War I, the Great Depression, and World War II. The witch never bothered the Bell family after that.

Still, even today, on dark and rainy nights, people have reported seeing strange lights gliding over fields near the Bell farm. Others have claimed to have heard the phantom sounds of people talking and children playing.

PULL OUT SLIDES 7 AND 8.
INSERT EACH SLIDE SEPARATELY INTO
YOUR 3-D GHOST VIEWER.

WHEN GHOSTS ATTACK

One of the biggest cases in the annals of paranormal history is the haunting and attack on Doris Bither by cruel spirits. The case was made into the blockbuster movie *The Entity* in 1981 and is now being remade by Hollywood producers for a future release.

THE ENTITIES

On August 22, 1974, Dr. Barry Taff and Kerry Gaynor arrived at 11547 Braddock Drive, the Culver City home of Doris Bither, a single mother of four children who ranged in age from 6 to 16.

Doris told investigators that she and her children had been abused by poltergeists. She also reported being slapped, thrown across the room, pinned down, and even bitten by these apparitions.

The paranormal investigators were at first skeptical of Bither. They believed that the troubled woman invited much of the "haunting" in her house through mental suggestion.

THE PROOF FINALLY APPEARS

The investigators soon quit doubting Bither's reports. Photographers, with high-speed cameras, were brought in to capture something on film. Doris conjured up the beings by calling out to them. To the investigators' surprise, lights began to manifest around the room.
A greenish mist swirled and grew in a corner. Within seconds, the form of a man's upper torso, large and heavily muscled, became visible in the mist. The eerie being had no facial details. An investigator reportedly fainted after witnessing this.

MOVING SPIRITS

Doris Bither moved from the house. She then reported that the cruel spirits "followed" her wherever she moved—and continued to taunt her. Dr. Barry Taff later wrote a book about the strange case.

By the late 1980s, the whereabouts of Doris Bither and her children were unknown.

PULL OUT SLIDES 9 AND 10.
INSERT EACH SLIDE SEPARATELY INTO
YOUR 3-D GHOST VIEWER.

THE LOST DUTCHMAN MINE

History is filled with stories of the greed of men, and how some are willing to kill for it. One of the most famous and mysterious stories is of the Lost Dutchman Mine, outside of Phoenix, Arizona.

SUPERSTITION MOUNTAINS

The name of the mine came from Jacob Walz, who was not a "Dutchman," but German. He came to America in 1845 and soon heard about the riches and adventure that were waiting in the undiscovered frontier land.

Around 1870, Walz's treasure-seeking brought him to the Arizona Territory. He disappeared into the Superstition Mountains to investigate local stories from Native Americans about gold. Soon, the "Dutchman" showed up in Phoenix with saddlebags full of gold.

Whenever anyone tried to get information out of him, he would always give false directions to the mine's location. Occasionally, men tried to follow Walz when he left town, but the prospector always disappeared in the mountains.

The "Dutchman" died on October 25, 1891, with a sack of rich gold ore beneath his deathbed. Would-be prospectors immediately sought what they called "The Lost Dutchman Mine" but never found it.

The search has caused more than a century of speculation. Theories as to the mine's location have filled dozens of books.

Hundreds of hopeful prospectors have searched the Superstition Mountain region. Some have returned empty-handed. Some have never returned...

GOLD DUST

WEIRD DEATHS

There is no way to guess just how many people have died trying to find the Lost Dutchman Mine—but it's definitely in the hundreds. Even Walz himself is alleged to have killed a few men who found his treasure trove or crossed him.

There are also many people who were slain by natives after they were found searching the mountain for the mine. Other deaths are more mysterious.

Many amateur and professional prospectors searching for the mine have disappeared. In some cases, their headless skeletons have been found; in others, bodies with bullet holes were found in shallow graves. From time to time, yet another person is reported missing in the area.

What has happened to them? It's a ghostly mystery— shrouded in as much secrecy as the Lost Dutchman mine itself.

GOLD FEVER
Top: Superstition Mountains.
Above: 19th century art of gold miners.

PULL OUT SLIDE 11 AND INSERT IT INTO YOUR 3-D GHOST VIEWER.

WAVERLY HILLS SANITARIUM

One of the most haunted places ever reported is the Waverly Hills Sanitarium in Louisville, Kentucky. There have been eyewitness reports of all kinds of paranormal activity – cold spots, disembodied voices, and apparitions roaming the halls. The large, abandoned, foreboding building has a dark and disturbing history.

THE EARLY DAYS

The Waverly Hills Sanitarium was built in 1910. Tuberculosis was so rampant in the ara that a separate building was constructed between 1924 and 1926. The treatment of tuberculosis was still in its early stages. Ten thousand patients of the sanitarium died within the first three years. It's estimated that 64,000 patients died by 1943. The hospital finally closed in 1961.

A year later, however, it reopened as the Woodhaven Geriatrics Sanitarium, where there have been many tales of patient mistreatment and unusual experiments. The state of Kentucky closed it in 1982 due to patient abuse.

HAUNTED HALLS

Well-known supernatural occurrences have been reported at the site. For example, the ghost of an old woman has often been seen running out the front door, her hands and legs chained and blood dripping from her wrists and ankles. She cries for help before she vanishes.

On the third floor of the building, many witnesses have seen a little girl known as "Mary," who plays with a ball. Some have seen the child peering out the third floor windows.

Other people have seen mysterious lights at night, even though the place has no electricity, or have heard voices that instructed them to "Get out."

PAIN AND MISERY

The general feeling of many investigators and visitors to the sanitarium is that of great despair. Often, places of great emotional pain and suffering are among the most haunted. It seems that Waverly Hills is no exception.

PULL OUT SLIDE 12 AND INSERT IT INTO YOUR 3-D GHOST VIEWER.

TWO GHOST SHIPS

Can you believe that a ship, with a dead and frozen crew, sailed for fourteen years by itself? It happened.

THE FROZEN DEAD

On the morning of October 11, 1775, the whaling ship *Herald* discovered a derelict boat, the *Octavius*, west of Greenland. The lifeless, three-masted schooner drifted among the icebergs in the North Atlantic.

Receiving no reply from his calls, Captain Warren and a small party of his sailors took a longboat over to the ghostly vessel and boarded her. What they found was terrifying. All members of the *Octavius* crew—more than 30 people—were frozen. Most of the crew lay in their bunks, perfectly preserved by the Arctic cold. The captain was found in his cabin, seated at his desk, pen still in hand.

LONG AT SEA

Captain Warren studied the dead captain's log. The last entry was made in 1761—fourteen years previous! The ship had left for China from England on September 10, 1761.

Spooked, Warren and his sailors went back to their ship. In the night, the wind and current carried away the *Octavius* and her dead crew. The three-masted schooner was never seen again.

Arguably the most famous of maritime mysteries is that of the *Mary Celeste*.

WHERE IS EVERYBODY?

The *Mary Celeste*, a brigantine merchant ship, was first found in the Atlantic Ocean in December 1872. Although the weather was fine, and her crew were experienced and able seamen, the phantom ship was abandoned. The *Mary Celeste* was in seaworthy condition, still under sail and heading toward the Strait of Gibraltar. She had been at sea for a month. The galley contained more than six months' worth of food and water. Her cargo was mostly untouched and the personal belongings of passengers and crew were still in place, including all valuables. The crew was never seen again.

THE STANLEY HOTEL

There have been numerous reports of haunted hotels all over the world. One haunted hotel has chilled guests with its eerie occurences and inspired a legendary horror author to write a blockbuster book based on the mysterious events that occurred in the ghostly place.

ROCKY MOUNTAIN RETREAT

The Stanley Hotel is a 138-room Georgian-style hotel located in the scenic Rocky Mountains of Colorado's Estes Park. Freelan Stanley, owner of Stanley Steamer automobiles, built the spacious lodge, which opened on July 4, 1909. Famous guests of the lavish hotel included many popular Hollywood celebrities and President Theodore Roosevelt.

HAUNTED HOTEL

The Stanley Hotel is believed to be haunted. Ghostly activity has been reported by the kitchen staff. The staff has repeatedly heard the sounds of parties and piano-playing coming from the ballroom, only to find the room empty. Others heard the ballroom piano being played but no one sitting at the instrument.

Some employees believe that the musician ghost is Freelan Stanley's wife, who used to be a piano player. Guests have reported seeing a man standing over their bed before running into the closet—often having stolen their jewelry or luggage.

In addition, the hotel founder, F.O. Stanley himself, has often been seen in the lobby and the Billiard Room, which was his favorite room when he was alive.

Paranormal investigators have claimed to witness ghostly occurrences, such as seeing apparitions appear in hallways and then hiding, hearing children running and playing on the floor above them, and seeing tables move all by themselves.

SHINING INSPIRATION

In the mid-1970s, horror author Stephen King and his wife stayed at the Stanley Hotel. The experience, and the talk of the hauntings at the hotel, inspired King to write his 1977 best-selling book *The Shining*.

The book was made into a hit film in 1980, which is shown daily at the hotel.

A popular TV movie adaptation of the book was filmed at the Stanley Hotel. Some of the action takes place in Room 217, where King began writing the novel.

HAUNTED HOTEL?

Top: The Hotel's massive concert hall, now used as a dining room.
Above: Vintage car on display in hotel lobby.

THE DEVON VISITOR

Have you ever been afraid of someone or something watching you from outside your bedroom window while you sleep? That is just what happened to the people of Devon, England, on February 9, 1855. It is one of the eeriest stories ever recorded.

THING IN THE NIGHT

On that fateful February morning, the people of Devon were surprised to find what appeared to be cloven hoofprints uniformly imprinted in the new-fallen snow.

The tracks, which measured 1.5 – 2.5 inches wide and eight inches apart, continued from the village out into the countryside for more than 100 miles. The tracks went up to stone walls, 18-foot-tall haystacks, over rooftops, through drain pipes, and across wide rivers.

No obstacle blocked the tracks. They appeared without interruption on the other side, as if the creature that made them moved through the obstacles.

Witnesses also noted that the tracks were set one in front of the other, suggesting that a biped, not a four-legged creature, had made them.

Who—or what—could make tracks that consistently traveled more than 100 miles on foot in the course of an evening?

THEORIES ABOUND

In addition to the tracks, some of the people reported seeing a "devil-like figure" in the area. Many people tried to disprove the existence of such a supernatural creature.

Some theories said that a weather balloon, dragging two strands of rope behind it, made the tracks. Others explained that it was "hopping mice" or, even more outlandishly, kangaroos that had escaped from a private zoo.

THE NIGHT THING RETURNS

On the night of March 12, 2009, more of the same hoofprints were discovered, just like those found back in 1855.

Could the thing that made those tracks—or a descendant—have returned to the village to watch the people of Devon slumber in the night?

Could it all have been some elaborate hoax? No one has been able to prove anything.

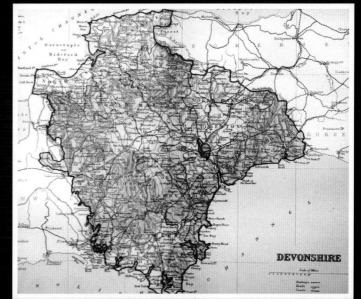

DEVONSHIRE

GLOSSARY

Apparition: A spirit in recognizably human form.

Entity: A spiritual being that may have been human once, but is no longer alive.

Intelligent Haunting: A haunting is deemed to be intelligent when a spirit is shown to interact or respond to those in the physical world. This is the opposite of a "residual haunting."

Manifestation: An event, action, or object that clearly shows or represents something, especially a theory or an abstract idea.

Orb: A ball or circle of light that is usually found in videos or photographs. Some believe that an orb is the energy or the spirit of an individual who has passed.

Paranormal: Events or occurrences that are beyond the range of normal scientific understanding.

Poltergeist: A ghost or other supernatural being supposedly responsible for physical disturbances such as loud noises and objects thrown around.

Residual Haunting: A haunting in which entities do not show awareness of the living world. Residual activity generally involves "playing back" routines from an entity's daily life. This is the opposite of an "intelligent haunting."

Shadow People: Mysterious dark shadows in human form that appear in pictures or video, but may be invisible to the naked eye. It is thought that these spirits do not have enough energy to materialize as full-bodied apparitions.

Supernatural: An event or a manifestation that is attributed to some force beyond scientific understanding or the laws of nature: a supernatural being.

True Life Hauntings   Copyright © 2010 Canopy Books

All rights reserved.

No part of this book may be reproduced, store in a retrieval system, or transmitted in any form or by any means, electronic, mechanical, photocopying, recording, or otherwise, without the prior permission of Canopy Books.

Produced by Canopy Books   www.cbproducts.com
50 Carnation Avenue, Floral Park, NY 11001
If you have any questions or comments about this product, please visit
www.cbproducts.com/contactus.html

Written by Don Roff
Book design and product development by Frank M. Young and Ryan Hobson
Production management by Paige Araujo

Image credits: pp. 1, 3 © Lena Pautina; p. 2: © Mike Sonnenberg; pp. 4, 7, 8, 10, 19, 22, 23: wikimedia.org; p. 5: top left, © www.trends-search.com; bottom right, © AmityvilleMurders.com; p. 6: © Shelli Peacock; p. 7: © Barry Wallis; p. 9:© J. Waters; p. 10: www.tnhistoryforkids.org; p. 11: © bellwitch.org; p. 12: © Gremlin; p. 13: © Pali Rao, Stratesigns, Inc.; p. 14: © Ivan Bajic, Dmitriy Norov, Mark Evans; p. 15: © Duncan Walker, Nick Boalch; pp. 16-17: © The Waverly Hills Historical Society Inc.; p. 18: © Linda Steward, Vasiliki Varvaki, Stanislav Pobytov p. 19: © Günter Jurczik, Yaroslav Bragin; p. 20: Sara Witte; p. 21: badu-zacchaeus.home4blogs.in, Shannon S. Valley; p. 23: www.antiquemaps.com/uk

Every effort has been made to correctly attribute all the material reproduced in this book. We will be happy to correct any errors in future editions.

Printed, manufactured, and assembled in China.

10 9 8 7 6 5 4 3 2 1